Thoughts On The Journey

by

Jean Temple

Bloomington, IN   authorHOUSE™   Milton Keynes, UK

AuthorHouse™
1663 Liberty Drive, Suite 200
Bloomington, IN 47403
www.authorhouse.com
Phone: 1-800-839-8640

AuthorHouse™ UK Ltd.
500 Avebury Boulevard
Central Milton Keynes, MK9 2BE
www.authorhouse.co.uk
Phone: 08001974150

First published by AuthorHouse 6/20/2006

ISBN: 1-4259-3608-3 (sc)

Printed in the United States of America
Bloomington, Indiana

This book is printed on acid-free paper.

Scripture quotations are from The Holy Bible, King James Versions

Dedication

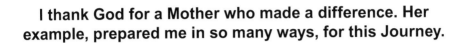

I thank God for a Mother who made a difference. Her example, prepared me in so many ways, for this Journey.

Acknowledgements

God has a way of placing just the right people
in your path. He has done that for me.
I am grateful to be part of a God-fearing,
Jesus-praising family.

Hallelujah!

I am grateful to have a husband
with great faith.

Special Acknowledgement

-- Alma, Lara, Shirley, Charlotte & Betty –

A very special Thank You.
Thank you for following your heart and
making my dream a reality.

**But seek ye first the kingdom of God,
and his righteousness; and all these
things shall be added unto you.**
Matthew 6:33

**Blessed are they that hear the word of God
and keep it.**
Luke 11:28

You Can Be Too Busy

**Putting God First can be challenging.
Don't let others make you feel guilty.
Be careful that you don't allow the small
or big stuff, out-stuff the God stuff.**

Thy Father which seeth in secret
shall reward thee openly.
Matthew 6:6

He that spared not his own Son, but
delivered him up for us all, how shall he
not with him also freely give us all things?
Romans 8:32

Too Many Blessings To Count

Why do we still ask for more?
God has given us more than we need.
What more, is there to ask for? The Lord has
Provided us with more than we deserve.

For the Lord God is a sun and shield:
the Lord will give grace and glory: no good thing
will He withhold from them that walk uprightly.
Psalms 84:11

He maketh His sun to rise on the evil and on the good,
and sendeth rain on the just and on the unjust.
Matthew 5:45

Can God Be Too Good?

The truth is: God is good.
We know that-- more than Good.
It is His sun and it was His Son.
Even the just are lacking, yet His
mercy and grace abounds.

Verily, verily, I say unto you,
He that heareth my word, and believeth on him that
sent me, hath everlasting life, and shall not come into
condemnation; but is passed from death unto life.
John 5:24

I go to prepare a place for you.
John 14:2

Homeward Bound

Realizing this earth is not our home and that God has prepared our home for us--and it's ready. It's finished, makes the Journey easier to bear during times of tribulation and trouble.

For what is a man profited, if he shall gain the whole world, and lose his own soul? Or what shall a man give in exchange for his soul?
Matthew 16:26

He that loveth his life shall lose it; and he that hateth his life in this world shall keep it unto life eternal.
John 12:25

Death

It appears that everyone wants to go to heaven,
yet no one wants to die to get there.

For this child I prayed; and the Lord hath given
me my petition which I asked of him: Therefore
also I have lent him to the Lord. As long as
he liveth he shall be lent to the lord.
I Samuel 1:27-28

And they said, Believe on the Lord Jesus Christ.
and thou shall be saved, and thy house.
Acts 16:31

Mama's Prayers

I can't count the times God has spared me, because of the prayers and obedience of my Mother. So much of our world is lost because Mothers have a different agenda – their own.

And he said, my presence shall go with thee, and I will give thee rest.
Exodus 33:14

Being confident of this very thing that he which hath begun a good work in you will perform it until the day of Jesus Christ.
Philippians 1:6

Lord, I'm So Tired

It's so easy to be pulled in so many directions. Distractions do just that. Just before I throw up my hands to give up on it all, the Spirit reminds me that God is with me, and because I am doing His work. He will renew my strength.

Ye are the light of the world.
A city that is set on a hill cannot be hidden.
Matthew 5:14.

Take my yoke upon you and learn of me; for I am meek
and lowly in heart: and ye shall find rest unto your souls.
Matthews 11:29.

Who gave himself for us, that he might redeem
us from all iniquity, and purify unto himself a
peculiar people, zealous of good works?
Titus 2:14

Me Lord?

I have asked myself more than once: Lord, do you really mean me? Soon, one learns, you really don't have an option. Yes, the Lord does mean you. He has told us; over and over again that we are His children, We are His light, we are His instruments, and we are His peculiar people.

When I said, my foot slippeth;
thy mercy, O Lord, held me up.
Psalms 94:18

And it shall come to pass, that before they call, I will
answer, and while they are yet speaking, I will hear.
Isaiah 65:24

Call unto me, and I will answer thee, and show thee
great and mighty things, which thou knowest not.
Jeremiah 33:3

Help

I need help so many times-the body wears out, the spirit gets weak--and when I have fallen, God is always there. Not one time has He failed to come to my rescue! I've often forgotten to call Him; you know, feeling like I can handle this without Him. I am so glad He knows me well enough that even in my blindness, He finds me, and extends just the help I need. For God is always with me.

But the Comforter, which is the Holy Ghost,
whom the Father will send in my name, he shall
teach you all things, and bring all things to your
remembrance, whatsoever I have said unto you.
John 14:26

Peace I leave with you, my peace I give unto you:
not as the world giveth, give I unto you. Let not
your heart be troubled, neither let it be afraid.
John 14: 27.

These things I have spoken unto you, that in me ye
might have peace. In the world ye shall have tribulation:
but be of good cheer; I have overcome the world.
John 16:33

Why Is This Happening To Me

Some days, you wonder why you got out of bed.
Then you remember that you did get out of bed!
You took your first breath of the day. Now trust
God. Whatever happened yesterday, happened.
God has blessed you with another day.
You get to start again.
You can't change yesterday.
You can go on from here!
Do something with this day that God has given you.
Because of Jesus, we can be victorious in all things.

Howbeit when he, the Spirit of truth, is come, he will guide you into all truth: for he shall not speak of himself; but whatsoever he shall hear, that shall he speak: and he will show you things to come.
John 16:13

My sheep hear my voice, and I know them, and they follow me.
John 10:27

Every one of us shall give account of himself to God.
Romans 14:12

Lord, Is That You?

When given some assignments, I have found myself double-checking God's Word to ensure this assignment is of God. I am ever so careful not to step into the traps that I know Satan has for me. Because the voice, of the critics can be so loud, I am caution to make sure I am in the Master's Will. The gentle reminder from the Holy Spirit affirms that I am in the right space. The critics are still there, but I am at peace with the assurance God's voice has provided. His voice actually becomes louder than the critics and nay-sayers. Doing the will of God becomes my will as I realize eternal life is sure to come.

With God nothing shall be impossible.
Luke 1:37

And they were healed every one.
Acts 4:10

The prayer of faith shall save the sick.
James 5:15

I Am Healed

One thing for sure, if you have not had a sick day, keep living, because a sick day is coming. Doctors (most, anyway) are a good thing and I thank God for the care, compassion that He has gifted them with. Yet, the longer I live, the more I realize that doctors are not all knowing. In fact they need us to pray for them. Pray that God will mix His divine miracle, working power with the human know-how for miracle cures. Prayer and faith are the prescription. Because I have taken this medicine: I am healed.

Put on the whole armor of God, that ye may be able to stand against the wiles of the devil.
Ephesians 6:11

And the God of peace shall bruise Satan under your feet shortly. The grace of our Lord Jesus Christ is with you. Amen.
Romans 16:20

For whatsoever is born of God overcometh the world; and this is the victory that overcometh the world, even our faith.
I John 5:4

The Devil Can't Bind Me.

One of Satan's goals is to stop any witness, or messenger of Christ. He has no shame, and will use anybody. Satan has no rulebook to follow, nothing is out of bounds for him, so whatever and whoever is available for His use, He'll use. You must be an over comer, suited up. The victory is already ours. Keep yourself free of the ropes that Satan would use to bind us. My armor is a permanent part of me. I sleep fully armed. I shower fully armed. I've got my armor on.

I am the door: by me if any man enter in,
he shall be saved.
John 10:9

Whosoever shall call on the name
of the Lord shall be saved.
Acts 2:1

The gift of God is eternal life through
Jesus Christ our Lord.
Romans 6:23

For by grace are ye saved through faith, and
that not of yourselves: it is the gift of God.
Ephesians 2:8

I'm Saved

How glad I am that God found me.
My blessing was that He found me while I was still
at a tender young age. I grew up knowing God as a
Father, who was able to supply all of my needs. The
greatest part of being saved is knowing that I am.

Ah, Lord God! Behold, thou hast made the heaven
and the earth by thy great power and stretched out
arms, and there is nothing too hard for thee.
Jeremiah 32:17

Alleluia: for the Lord God omnipotent reigneth.
Revelation 19:6

Great and marvelous are thy works Lord God Almighty.
Revelation 15:3

Only God

When thoughts come out of nowhere, and answers to questions are on the tip of your tongue for subjects that are foreign to you, your heart whispers softly "Only God". When dangers, spiritual and physical, are all around you and you are still untouched by it all, again the spirit reveals "Only God". When your ears have been deafened so the lies, and the gossip are not heard by you, you truly know "Only God."

If ye abide in me, and my words abide in you,
ye shall ask what ye will, and it shall be done unto you.
John 15:7

And this is the confidence that we have in him, that, if
we ask anything according to his will, he heareth us;
and if we know that he hear us, whatsoever we ask, we
know that we have the petitions that we desired of him. *I
John 5:14-15*

They that are with Him are called,
and chosen, and faithful.
Revelation 17:14

Getting Out Of The Boat

Often times God made the boat uncomfortable,
rocky and stormy so my faith walk was a choice
with some encouragement. Knowing the Lord
is always with me and whatever he has given me
to do makes it possible to get out of the boat.
This book is an out-of-the boat experience.

Even As A Child

**And all the children shall be taught of the Lord;
and great shall be the peace of thy children.**
Isaiah 54:13

**Suffer the little children to come unto me,
and forbid them not: for of such is the kingdom of God.**
Mark 10:14

Even As a Child

God came to my rescue early. Even as a child, the enemy tried to kill me. He didn't have a chance. A praying grandmother and mother kept me alive, as they nursed me, and held me each night to keep me from dying from a chronic breathing disorder. God gave them wisdom and guidance, and satan lost again. God will watch over your children. Pray to Him for the wisdom that you need, and He will guide you.

**Blessed are they that do
his commandments that they may have
the right to the tree of life.**
Revelation 22:14

**Let no man despise thy youth;
but be thou an example of the believers, in word,
in conversation, in charity, in spirit, in faith, in purity.**
I Timothy 4:12

A Great Story Teller

Mom is a great storyteller. She has helped me to remember by retelling my childhood stories over and over. I am sure that God has used her as a gentle yet stern reminder of the work He had for me to do. Be Busy doing what God has for you.

**Commit thy way unto the Lord;
trust also in him; and he shall bring it to pass.**
Psalms 37:5

God is Light, and in him there is not darkness at all.
I John 1:5

Life Experiences

My life experiences have served to bond my personal relationship with the Lord. Each deliverance, each victory, reconfirmed that I need to be His witness--be another believer that will bring light in our dire, dark world. Life begins when we begin to walk in the light of God.

Let the words of my mouth and the meditation
of my heart, be acceptable in thy sight, O
Lord, my strength, and my redeemer.
Psalms 19:14

Then the king commanded, and they brought
Daniel, and cast him into the den of lions. Now the
king spake and said unto Daniel, Thy God whom
thou servest continually, he will deliver thee.
Daniel 6:16

I have fought a good fight, I have finished
my course, I have kept the faith.
II Timothy 4:7

The Journey

I have finally come to understand that the Journey is not about you or me. It's about Christ. The Journey is not about how you feel, what your agenda or thoughts are as they relate to God's work. The Journey is about Christ. Not who you are or who you know, not the titles you have or aspire to gain, not your family or friends, your finances or lack of. It's all about God, His work, His agenda and your assignment.
You do have an assignment.

Let us run with patience the race that is set before us.
Hebrews 12:1

Ye have not chosen me, but I have chosen you.
John 15:16

But ye are a chosen generation a royal priesthood, an holy nation, a peculiar people; that ye should show forth the praises of him who hath called you out of darkness into his marvelous light.
I Peter 2:9

Destiny

I am convinced that God has predestined a path for all of His children to walk. God has a purpose of all of us. If He woke you up this morning, it's because your work is still incomplete. He still has more work for you to finish. Get busy be in the Will of God. If you want peace, fulfill your Destiny.

Therefore said he unto them, The harvest truly
is great, but the labourers are few: pray ye
therefore the Lord of the harvest, that he would
send forth labourers into his harvest.
Luke 10:2

For, brethren, ye have been called unto liberty;
only use not liberty for an occasion to the flesh,
but by love serve one another
Galatians 5:13

Still Searching

Christians have approached me on several occasions with these questions. What is my destiny? How will I know when I find it? First, I tell them that you must realize your destiny is not lost, you are. You are lost or blind to what God has placed right in front of you. Look around your local Church--there is work to do. How is it possible for there to be so much work, and yet Christians are still searching. It's truly sad. Some Christians will never find, or at least never acknowledge, what God's plan is for their lives because God's plan is different than theirs. We serve such a gracious, matchless, God. He will not force His will upon any of his children. It's our free will that gets us in trouble. I have learned to trade my free will for God's will. The journey is a lot easier having done so.

The counsel of the Lord standeth forever.
Psalms 33:11

Not that we are sufficient of ourselves to think any thing of ourselves; but our sufficiency is of God.
II Corinthians 3:5

God is greater than our heart, and knoweth all things.
I John 3:20

God Has The Best Plan

God has carefully planned our lives. Each step along this journey prepares us for the next step ahead, all working toward our ultimate fulfillment in God's master plan. Once we understand this principle, we can take each step in faith and walk with confidence, knowing that God is in control; that we are in His will--His master plan. We are in the hands of the Master who already knows the outcomes to all our future encounters. Let go and let God do it.

The spirit of God hath made me,
and the breath of the Almighty hath given me life.
Job 33:4

But God commendeth his love toward us in that,
while we were yet sinners, Christ died for us.
Romans 5:8

Ye are bought with a price; be not
ye the servants of men.
I Corinthians 7:23

Purchased Indeed

The Journey is all about waking each day, knowing that Christ has made our life worth living. Our life has been brought to us by Christ; thereby to live a life that is pleasing to our Savior should become our purpose and goal. Life goes better with Christ.

Reflections

O Lord my God, I will give thanks unto thee forever.
Psalms: 30:12

My cup runneth over.
Psalms 23:5

I was glad when they said unto me,
Let us go into the house of the Lord.
Psalms 122:1

Reflections

When I look back over my life, I understand that God has commissioned me to write my story so others would come to know Him. I have so much to be Thankful for, the pages would not hold the many blessings God has made possible in my life. Life experiences have taught me that God is able. The victories have been a constant reminder of His faithfulness. I now can embrace the Journey full of faith.

If I ascend up into heaven, thou art there: if I make my bed in hell, behold, thou art there.
Psalms 139:8

In my Father's house are many mansions.
John 14:2

Lord, Thou art God, which hast made heaven, and earth, and the sea.
Acts 4:24

I saw a new heaven and a new earth: for the first heaven and the first earth were passed away.
Revelation 21:1

Heaven

Heaven is real.
Either you believe the Word of God or you don't.
If you are a believer, then know there is a payday
coming. Our Father is writing your check,
whatever is right, will be your pay.
Heaven is real.

Hell hath enlarged herself, and opened
her mouth without measure.
Isaiah 5:14

The fire that never shall be quenched.
Mark 9:45

Between us and you there is a great gulf fixed:
so that they which would pass from hence to you
cannot.
Luke 16:26.

Hell

Hell is real.
There is life after death.
You need to make the right decisions on your
journey so you don't end up in hell.

A new heart also will I give you,
and a new spirit will I put within you.
Ezekiel 36:26

Jesus answered and said unto him, Verily,
verily, I say unto thee, Except a man be born
again, he cannot see the kingdom of God.
John 3:3

He shall give you another Comforter, that
he may abide with you forever.
John 14:16

The Holy Spirit Is REAL

The Holy Spirit is real, and will live within if you let Him.
The Spirit is there to lead you, if you let Him
The Spirit is there to walk with you, if you let Him.
The Spirit is there to speak for you, if you let Him.
The Spirit will be real in your life if you let Him.

If Thou be the Son of God, come down from the cross.
Matthew 27:40

He bearing his cross went forth.
John 19:17

God forbid that I should glory, save in
the cross of our Lord Jesus Christ.
Galatians: 6:14

The Cross Is REAL

The story is an old one-yet the telling of it still brings, a hush within. Christ bore the ultimate Cross--so we could handle these small crosses we encounter on the Journey. If you ever think your cross is too much for you to bear, think about the size of the Cross Jesus bore that Friday--the one with your and my sins on it. Keep the Cross-real; it will make the Journey much easier to bear.

The Blood Christ Shed Is REAL

Without the shedding of blood is no remission.
Hebrews 9:22

The blood of Jesus Christ his Son
cleanseth us from all sin.
I John 1:7

Worthy is the Lamb that was slain.
Revelation 5:12

The Blood Christ Shed Is REAL

The Blood had to be real;
without it, there would be no grace, no mercy,
no salvation, and no me.

Ye are the temple of the living God.
II Corinthians 6:16

I will have mercy on whom I will have mercy,
and compassion on whom I will have compassion.
Romans 9:15

God knoweth your hearts.
Luke 16:15

Women

Everyone has an opinion about women and ministry; where do we fit, where do we belong. The truth is YOUR opinion does not count. Each of us, need to make sure that our Journeys are in step with what the Lord would have for our lives. If we could move "self" out of the way, we would know the truth. God's plan is not our plan. Quit trying to figure it out for everyone else. It will take a huge effort just to get it right for you. If we just let God speak to our hearts, satan would not have another weapon to use on God's children.

Thy loving-kindness is better than life.
Psalms 63:3

I will never leave thee, nor forsake thee.
Hebrews 13:5

For God so loved the world, that he gave his only begotten Son, that whosoever believeth in him should not perish, but have everlasting life.
John 3:16

Lord, You Love Me?

To realize that God cares about me is enough to help me face the challenges of this Journey. To realize wherever I am, He has promised to be with me, that He will not leave me, even in my wrongness. His love is matchless, and the demonstration of His love is constant.

Ye are the salt of the earth: but if the salt has lost his savour, wherewith shall it be salted? It is thenceforth good for nothing, but to be cast out, and to be trodden under foot of men.
Matthew 5:13

The night is far spent, the day is at hand: let us therefore cast off the works of darkness and let us put on the armor of light.
Romans 13:12

And let us not be weary in well doing: for in due season we shall reap, if we faint not.
Galatians 6:9

Bench Warmers

So many Christians today are silent, satisfied sitting back. Stale. They may know that God is indeed real; however, they can't or won't share it even with those they love. Be assured that our Lord is still calling men and women to do His work. When you reflect on the Greatness of God, what He has done for you, how can you remain on the bench? Get Up!

God is our refuge and strength, a
very present help in trouble.
Psalms 46:1

Behold, I am the Lord, the God of all flesh:
is there any thing too hard for me
Jeremiah 32:27

Casting all your care upon him; for he careth for you.
I Peter 5:7

Baby Steps

I can trust God to take care of me. Even when I can't speak for myself, the Lord has spoken for me. I took several baby steps to get to that level of faith. I continually thank Him now, as I can recall the many foolish attempts to come to my own defense, when I was doing as the Master commanded. He will handle His own business; God only needs us to step back, so we don't get knocked down in the process. Step Back.

We were in our own sight as grasshoppers.
Numbers 13:33

The battle is the Lord's.
I Samuel 17:47

Our God shall fight for us.
Nehemiah 4:20

If God Be for us, who can be against us?
Roman 8:31

Living With Giants

I recall my early years at Angel Elementary School-- it was a traumatic experience. I didn't talk much, so my second grade teacher assumed I was retarded. Assumptions are dangerous things. My teacher's assumptions caused her to respond to me differently, which caused me to draw even farther away. The Giants can be mean creatures. Yet you can survive in a world where everyone is bigger, louder and stronger than you. Even though I felt like a grasshopper, the Lord made up the difference. He will protect you from the Giants of this world. He always does.

Great is thy faith: be it unto thee even as thou wilt.
Matthews 15:28

Have faith in God.
Mark 11:22

**Faith should not stand in the wisdom of men,
but in the power of God.**
I Corinthians 2:5

Just A Little Bit Of Faith

Just a little bit of faith goes a long way. It's like God can see that you are trying. His Son is standing on His right side, cheering us on. The Lord has our miracle. He has the solution to our problems. He is just waiting for you to put your faith in action.

A Little that a righteous man hath is better
than the riches of many wicked.
Psalms 37:16

There is that maketh himself rich, yet hath nothing:
there is that maketh himself poor, yet hath great riches.
Proverbs 13:7

What shall it profit a man, if he shall gain the
whole world, and lose his own soul?
Mark 8:36

Set your affections on things above,
not on things on the earth.
Colossians 3:2

To Be Rich

I recall days when I would dream of having all the money that I wanted. I would list the things that I would do first: like take care of my Mom, buy a house, and make sure my nieces and nephews had money for college. I would build a mansion where all my family could live so we would be close, but in our own separate homes. I would give to charities, give to medical research, the list goes on and on. I'm not sure at what age I realized that I was already rich. Not like the world might judge, but rich still, rich indeed. I have the love of Jesus, and His love gives me more riches than money could buy. This is a richness that I can share, and never have to worry that God's Love will run out, no one could steal it, misuse it. The value of His Love does not change with the Dow Jones or inflation. I have it, and I am rich.

It hath pleased the Lord to make you his people.
I Samuel 12:22

But God commendeth his love toward us, in that, while we were yet sinners, Christ died for us.
Romans 5:8

Ye are all the children of God by faith in Christ Jesus.
Galatians 3:26

Chosen

These thoughts have been rattling around in my heart and mind since I heard my mother say them. We were chosen by God to do a special work. Don't expect those who have not been chosen to understand the work or the mission God has chosen for you to do. When you have the full understanding of what a privilege it is to be chosen by God, you can then rejoice. So when people talk about you think "chosen". When your friends lie about you, think "chosen". When you are doing your best and you are misunderstood, think "chosen". When you think no one loves you, think "Chosen".

In the beginning God created the heaven and the earth.
Genesis 1:1

And God made two great lights, the greater light to rule the day, and the lesser light to rule the night: he made the stars also. And God set them in the firmament of the heaven to give light upon the earth, And to rule over the day and over the night, and to divide the light from the darkness: and God saw that it was good.
Genesis 1:16-18

Running Out of Time

Life has become so busy; each day is filled with more than should fit in any 24-hour day. I know that God does all things well. If the day gets done before all you have planned, then not only have you planned too much, but you are too busy. God gave us enough time to praise and worship Him each day. ALL that really matters is that within the 24 hours He has provided, we praise, and we worship. Run out of time when it comes to the other stuff, but never lose sight of who gave us this day. God is the only one making days, so remember to include Him in yours.

God is my salvation; I will trust, and not be afraid.
Isaiah 12:2

I am the door: by me if any man
enter in, he shall be saved.
John 10:9

Whosoever shall call on the name
of the Lord shall be saved.
Acts 2:21

That if thou shalt confess with thy mouth the Lord
Jesus, and shalt believe in thine heart that God hath
raised him from the dead, thou shalt be saved.
Romans 10:9

Feelings

I'm so glad that salvation is not based on a feeling. There are days I don't feel I'm saved. Don't misunderstand me; I know I am saved, yet with the stuff of this world, job, family, friends, sickness, I may not feel it. That's why I am so glad my salvation is not based on how I feel. What a wonderful revelation, to know my salvation is secure in the promise of God and the belief He has sealed in my heart.

Deceive not yourselves.
Jeremiah 37:9

Take heed that ye be not deceived.
Luke 21:8

Beware lest any man spoil you through
philosophy and vain deceit.
Colossians 2:8

Running Away

It's a sad thing, but the truth is I've seen Christians move their membership from church to church. Many of them justifying their moves based upon some experience, or lack of experience, with some other Christian. I don't think I have ever met one who "church hopped" because of themselves, it was always the actions or lack of action by another. I have watched how Satan has deceived many, my counsel has always been, know that you are in a church that is preaching the truth of the Gospel. After that you need to look within. Most folks are deceived by the enemy to leave the church they love. The problems and confusion they left show up again at their new Church, because the problems were internal within themselves. Stop running. Satan will have you run, so you never stay in one place, to really face and deal with YOU.

The Lord bless thee, and keep thee: The
Lord make his face shine upon thee, and
be gracious unto thee: The Lord lift up his
countenance upon thee, and give thee peace.
Numbers 6:24-26

Behold I set before you this day a blessing and a
curse; A blessing, if ye obey the commandments
of the Lord your God, which I command you
this day: and a curse, if ye will not obey
Deuteronomy 11:26-28

Blessed shalt thou be in the city, and
blessed shalt thou be in the field.
Deuteronomy 28:3

Counting Blessings

The many blessings we take for granted:
The Sun: For the sunlight and heat
The Moon: To guide us by night where
there are no streetlights.
The Stars: for their beauty and the hope that
causes us to look above toward heaven.
The Air: That has never run out, it's always there.
The Green Grass: For cows to graze.
The Clouds in the Sky: To remind us
that there is a heaven above.
The Rain: that keeps our crops growing for food.
Oranges: For vitamin C.
Apples Trees: For their beautiful bloom and fruit.
Dogs: Pets that listen, when people would not.

Every one that asketh receiveth.
Matthews 7:8

Hitherto have ye asked nothing in my name: ask, and ye shall receive, that your joy may be full.
John 16:24

Counting Blessings (Continued...)

And still there's more--so many that I can't count.
God has not only blessed me personally, but He has
blessed mankind.   I know I don't deserve what He has
already done, for I have left undone so much that He
has asked me to do. Yet, He keeps on blessing me.
Thank you Lord for mercy and grace that
does not run out, because of your grace
and mercy you continue to bless me.
I thank you.

It is finished.
John 19:30

And said, Behold, I see the heavens opened and the Son of man standing on the right hand of God.
Acts 7:56

Shortly I must put off this my tabernacle.
II Peter 1:14

Last Words

I don't know what my last words will be. I know my thoughts will be centered between heaven and earth. Earth: My concern for those that I have left in life, if the Rapture has not come, to continue it without me. Heaven: For the Savior that is waiting to meet me, and all the souls and spirits that have gone on before me.

**Train up a child in the way he should go:
and when he is old, he will not depart from it.**
Proverbs 22:6

Honour they father and thy mother.
Matthew 19:19

**The children ought not to lay up for the parents,
but the parents for the children.**
2 Corinthians 12:14

Mothers

Mom, if you have not gotten it by now, is a special lady. Her eyes still light up when she talks about her children, even though we are now adults with families of our own. She never lets a birthday go by without celebration. Mom makes all of us feel special and unique. She respects our differences for the gifts God has given each of her children.

Thou shalt find him, if thou seek him
with all thy heart and with all they soul.
Deuteronomy 4:29

All have sinned, and come short of the glory of God.
Roman 3:23

God is no respecter of persons.
Acts 10:34

Seek those things which are above,
where Christ sitteth on the right hand of God.
Colossians 3:1

The Beginning

In the beginning, during my baby days in Christ, I was a mess. As I reflect over these years, I realize now just how much Christ had to come to my rescue. The enemy had his demons everywhere, even in the church It's so easy to get caught up in church politics or "churchin". The enemy is on his job; he will do whatever he can to keep you from the fellowship of saints, and witnessing. Because you are a babe in Christ, you may not see the enemy coming. He'll look just like church folks, all dressed but he's the devil in sheep's clothing. I had some narrow escapes. I learned to pray on this Journey. More prayers are needed at the beginning. Get in a prayer circle or with a prayer warrior--one that will be in constant prayer for you. The enemy will flee; the prayers of the righteous will make you and Christ a team. The enemy will search for other babes in Christ that don't know this key and leave you alone.

Thou art my hope, O Lord God:
Thou art my trust from my youth.
Psalms 71:5

We are saved by hope.
Romans 8:24

We are perplexed, but not in despair; persecuted,
but not forsaken: cast down, but not destroyed.
II Corinthians 4:8-9

Hope

God has blessed me with the gift of hope-- I realize that now, as He shows me hope in all situations. I know He is able to do all things. Even in the darkest hours, when others have lost hope, I hold on to Christ, His promises, and His word. I wait for His answer. I have learned to put my trust in Him, not in the economy, the bank, doctors or the legal system. Put your hope in Christ Jesus; He is the only sure thing!

Heal me, O Lord and I shall be healed;
save me, and I shall be saved
Jeremiah 17:14

And they were healed every one.
Act 5:16.

He had faith to be healed
Acts 14:9

Healing

When I was diagnosed with a major skin disorder caused by the sun, it took three years for the doctors to find out what was causing the pain and skin breakouts. I had gotten used to being in pain and really could not remember what it felt like to be free of pain. Then one Saturday morning I awoke, and the pain was gone. It took a few minutes for me to really grasp the miracle--no pain. God had heard my prayers.

My salvation shall be for ever,
and my righteousness shall not be abolished.
Isaiah 51:6

Salvation is of the Lord.
Jonah 2:9

I go to prepare a place for you.
John 14:2

The wages of sin is death; but the gift of God
is eternal life through Jesus Christ our Lord.
Romans 6:23

Insurance

Who would think of living this life without insurance? Some do, and it takes them several years to recover their losses when they face crises without insurance. But, at least they recover. Should you dare to live this life without accepting the assurance in the Blood of Christ, you will never recover. Your life would be lost forever.

I will not return with thee:
for thou hast rejected the word of the Lord.
I Samuel 15:26

If thou forsake him, he will cast thee off for ever.
I Chronicle 28:9

He came unto his own, and his own received him not.
John 1:11

Whom he hath sent him ye believe not.
John 5:38

Rejections

It was a Journey experience that gave me the revelation of who I was in Christ. Knowing that God made me has provided such strength, as mankind still rejects what they cannot understand or control. My assurance of acceptance comes from the Creator; I no longer seek approval from man. Hallelujah!

Give me understanding, and I shall live.
Psalms 119:144

In him we live, and move and have our being.
Acts 17:28

Let the peace of God rule in your hearts.
Colossians 3:15

Now we live, if ye stand fast in the Lord.
Thessalonians 3:8

Life Goes On

I've had some days that I needed to convince myself
that there was a reason to continue this Journey: my
brother's murder, life disappointments, just the events
of this troubled world. Yet tomorrow has come, and
the Lord has delivered. He brings peace in the midst
of confusion. I know I could not have lived my life
without Jesus. I know there were situations in my
life; I came through because of the Lord's Son.
Thank You God for sending your Son,
so He could send the Comforter.

Show them the way wherein
they must walk, and the work that they must do.
Exodus 18:20

Where no counsel is, the people fall.
Proverbs 11:14

Whosoever will be chief among you,
let him be your servant.
Matthew 20:27

He that is greatest among you shall be your servant.
Matthew 23:11

Leaders

Being a leader is what I do, but not what I desired. I have learned to put my will in line with that of the Master. If you want to be a leader, stay humble, the Lord will lift you up. He uses those who are sure not to take the glory for themselves.

He giveth power to the faint; and to them that
have no might he increaseth strength.
Isaiah 40:29

God hath chosen the weak things of the world
to confound the things which are mighty.
I Corinthians 1:27

When I am weak, then am I strong.
II Corinthians 12:10

Weakness

Coming to grips with my weakness was a tough job. I discovered that the only way I could gain strength in these areas was first to acknowledge they existed. When I realize those areas in which I have weaknesses, I actually gain power, because now I have a choice. I could remain weak or chart a course that would make me strong.

God is my strength and power: and
he maketh my way perfect.
II Samuel 22:33

God is the strength of my heart, and my portion forever.
Psalms 73:26

Though our outward man perish,
yet the inward man is renewed day by day.
II Corinthians 4:16

Be strong in the Lord, and in the power of his might.
Ephesians 6:10

Strength

Sometimes, I surprise myself; my self-talk is I don't know where the strength comes from. My reality is that I absolutely know that my strength comes from the Lord. When those who have injured my heart feel they are so self-righteous, the spirit within is stronger still. It's a little scary, when you encounter the revelation that as long as you are in the Lord's Will, He will give you strength.

And they shall be one flesh.
Genesis 2:24

Rejoice with the wife of thy youth.
Proverb 5:18

What therefore God hath joined together,
let not man put asunder.
Mark 10:9

He that loveth his wife loveth himself.
Ephesians 5:28

Teach the young women to be sober to love
their husbands, to Love their children.
Titus 2:4

Marriage

I woke the day after my wedding, and wondered what had I done. I was so excited about the marriage, that I had not given much thought to the security I was leaving, home with a mother and a father, food, shelter, etc. always were there. We were young and had a lot to learn about living. I soon learned that God had given me all that I needed. It took some time for us to really become the one flesh that God intended, but we did and we are.

A good man showeth favour, and lendeth.
Psalm 112:5

He that watereth shall be watered also himself.
Proverbs 11:25.

The love of money is the root of all evil.
I Timothy 6:10

The care of this world, and the deceitfulness
of riches, choke the word.
Matthew 13:22

Finances

My dad taught me this posture about lending money. He summed it up this way. Don't lend what you can't afford to lose. When you lend money, don't expect it back, so if it returns to you from the lendee count it as a blessing. Be a Blessing.

The voice of him that crieth in the wilderness.
Isaiah 40:3

They shall declare my glory among the Gentiles.
Isaiah 66:19

He that taketh not his cross, and followeth
after me is not worthy of me.
Matthew 10:38

Whosoever will come after me let him deny
himself, and take up his cross, and follow me.
Mark 8:34

Follow me.
John 21:19

Disciples

Lord teach me to be the disciple that is needed in this day and age, to do Kingdom building work. Help me stay the course that you have laid in front of me. Hold back the distractions of all those well meaning Christians, who are your children, but are not disciples yet. I know they don't understand my course. Continue to bless me with the strength I need to help them and defeat the enemy.
Amen.

About the Author

"Thoughts on the Journey" is my first published work. I have spoken at many conferences, seminars around the County. I am often asked by those in attendance to share more about myself, views, and how I became the person I am., followed by several request for copies of my talk, presentation etc. So often, my thoughts are just that, inspired by the precious Holy Spirit that God had blessed me in, thought or with. This first publication is a "promised kept" to many whose paths I have cross and to God, who I promised that I would share, my life lessons, stories in to order to be a help to others.

Made in the USA
Middletown, DE
13 June 2023